Friendship Rocks

FRIENDS LISTEN

by **Megan Borgert-Spaniol**

PEBBLE
a capstone imprint

Published by Pebble, an imprint of Capstone.
1710 Roe Crest Drive
North Mankato, Minnesota 56003
capstonepub.com

Library of Congress Cataloging-in-Publication Data
Names: Borgert-Spaniol, Megan, 1989- author.
Title: Friends listen / Megan Borgert-Spaniol.
Description: North Mankato : Pebble, 2022. | Series: Friendship rocks | Includes bibliographical references and index. | Audience: Ages 5-8 | Audience: Grades K-1 | Summary: "Everyone's view counts. We all want our thoughts and feelings to be acknowledged by others. A good friend listens to what we have to say. This means being open and encouraging while not interrupting or judging. Learn how to be a good friend by being a good listener!"— Provided by publisher.
Identifiers: LCCN 2021029957 (print) | LCCN 2021029958 (ebook) | ISBN 9781666315561 (hardcover) | ISBN 9781666320107 (paperback) | ISBN 9781666315622 (pdf) | ISBN 9781666315745 (kindle edition)
Subjects: LCSH: Friendship—Juvenile literature. | Listening—Juvenile literature.
Classification: LCC BF575.F66 B666 2022 (print) | LCC BF575.F66 (ebook) | DDC 177/.62—dc23
LC record available at https://lccn.loc.gov/2021029957
LC ebook record available at https://lccn.loc.gov/2021029958

Editorial and Design Credits
Editor: Jessica Rusick, Mighty Media; Designer: Aruna Rangarajan, Mighty Media

Image Credits
iStockphoto: kali9, Cover; Shutterstock: Africa Studio, 13, Air Images, 15, Comeback Images, 9, fizkes, 7, Iam_Anupong, 5, InesBazdar, 16, 17, Lucky Business, 11, lunamarina, 21, Rido, 19, Sudowoodo, 20

Design Elements: Mighty Media, Inc.

All internet sites appearing in back matter were available and accurate when this book was sent to press.

TABLE OF CONTENTS

Words in **bold** are in the glossary.

Are You Listening?

You are at school. Your friend finds you. He starts talking about his weekend camping trip. But you are thinking about lunch.

You hear your friend talking. But you are not listening. Listening is paying **attention** to what someone says. It also means thinking about what you hear.

Listen with Your Body

Can you tell when your friend isn't listening? Maybe she is playing while you talk. You might feel like she doesn't care.

You can show a friend you are listening. Stop what you are doing. Turn to face your friend. Look her in the eyes.

Listen with Your Mind

You might look like you are listening. But what if you are thinking about something else? Then you are not really listening.

To listen, you have to pay attention. Think about what your friend says. Try to understand how he feels. Ask him questions about his story.

Check Back

Your friend hurt his arm. He tells you he got hurt playing hockey. You think about how he must feel. You ask if he needs help carrying his books.

Later, you ask your friend how his arm feels. This shows you were listening to him. It also shows that you care!

Work Together

Listening helps you work with others. Your friends might have ideas you wouldn't.

You and your friends are building a fort. You want to build one with pillows. But this doesn't work. Your friend has the idea to use blankets. Her idea works!

Listen and Learn

Listening to others lets you learn new things. You and your friend go to the beach. Your friend knows a lot about the ocean. He loves to learn about it! You ask your friend to share what he's learned. Now you know more than you did before!

Everyone's Voice Matters

You and your friend are working on a class **project**. Your friend shares an idea. You also have an idea to share. But don't **interrupt** your friend!

Listen as she speaks. Let her finish speaking before you talk. Make sure to **consider** both her idea and yours!

Ready to Listen

Sometimes we feel too busy to listen. Your friend is telling you about her new game. But you are trying to do homework.

You ask your friend if you can talk later. After you finish your homework, you find your friend. You are ready to listen. You learn all about her new game!

Practice Listening

Practice listening with your body and mind! Show your friend you are listening by remembering what they said.

WHAT YOU DO:

1. Sit facing your friend. Ask them what they did yesterday.

2. Sit still while your friend talks. Think about what they say.

3. When your friend is done talking, try to remember what they said. Write down everything you remember.

4. Switch places so your friend can practice listening too.

Glossary

attention (uh-TEN-shuhn)—careful listening or watching

consider (kuhn-SI-duhr)—to think about something

interrupt (in-tuh-RUHPT)—to start talking before someone else has finished talking

project (PRO-jekt)—a school assignment that students work on over a period of time

Read More

Ludwig, Trudy. *Quiet Please, Owen McPhee!* New York: Alfred A. Knopf, 2018.

Rossiter, Brienna. *Being Kind at School.* Lake Elmo, MN: Focus Readers, 2021.

Sauer, Tammi. *Wordy Birdy.* New York: Doubleday Books for Young Readers, 2018.

Internet Sites

KidsHealth—Mindfulness
kidshealth.org/en/kids/mindfulness.html?WT.ac=ctg#cathelp-yourself

PBS Kids—Arthur: Inside the Ear
pbskids.org/video/arthur/3001451080

Wonderopolis—What Does It Mean to Be a Good Friend?
wonderopolis.org/index.php/wonder/what-does-it-mean-to-be-a-good-friend

Index

About the Author

Megan Borgert-Spaniol is an author and editor of children's media. When she isn't writing or reading, she enjoys doing yoga, eating croissants, and crafting homemade pizzas. Megan lives in Minneapolis, Minnesota, with a tall, goofy man and a small, chatty cat.